# HEROIC ★ JOBS

# MOUNTAIN RESCUE

## Chris Oxlade

Raintree

**www.raintreepublishers.co.uk**
Visit our website to find out more information about Raintree books.

**To order:**
☎ Phone 0845 6044371
📄 Fax +44 (0) 1865 312263
💻 Email myorders@raintreepublishers.co.uk

Customers from outside the UK please telephone +44 1865 312262

Raintree is an imprint of **Capstone Global Library Limited**, a company incorporated in England and Wales having its registered office at 7 Pilgrim Street, London, EC4V 6LB – Registered company number: 6695582.

Text © Capstone Global Library Limited 2012
First published in hardback in 2012
Paperback edition first published in 2013

Edited by Dan Nunn, Rebecca Rissman, and Catherine Veitch
Designed by Joanne Malivoire
Picture research by Elizabeth Alexander
Originated by Capstone Global Library
Printed and bound in China by CTPS

ISBN 978 1 406 23208 0 (hardback)
15 14 13 12 11
10 9 8 7 6 5 4 3 2 1

ISBN 978 1 406 23215 8 (paperback)
16 15 14 13 12
10 9 8 7 6 5 4 3 2 1

**British Library Cataloguing in Publication Data**
Oxlade, Chris.
Mountain rescue. – (Heroic jobs)
363.1'481-dc22
A full catalogue record for this book is available from the British Library.

**Acknowledgements**
We would like to thank the following for permission to reproduce photographs: Alamy pp. 4 (© FORGET Patrick/SAGAPHOTO.COM), 6 (© Alaska Stock), 8 (© Caro), 9 (© FORGET Patrick/SAGAPHOTO.COM), 10 (© Ashley Cooper), 11 (© FORGET Patrick/SAGAPHOTO. COM), 14 (© Ashley Cooper), 19 (© blickwinkel), 20 (© Francesco Gavazzeni), 21 (© South West Images Scotland), 23 (© Ashley Cooper pics), 24 (© GAUTIER Stephane/SAGAPHOTO.COM), 26 (© Ashley Cooper), 29 (© Jeff Morgan 01); Corbis p. 16 (© John Van Hasselt); Photolibrary pp. 5 (Patrick Forget/Saga Photo), 7 (Matt Hage/Alaskastock), 12 (Patrick Forget/Saga Photo), 13 (Patrick Forget/Saga Photo), 15 (Patrick Forget/Saga Photo), 17 ( Patrick Forget/Saga Photo), 22 (Hermes Images/Tips Italia), 27 (UWL/Imagebroker.net); Photoshot p. 25 (Paul Freytag); Shutterstock p. 18 (© amidala76).

Cover photograph of a rescuer searching for avalanche survivors reproduced with permission of Alamy (© FORGET Patrick/SAGAPHOTO.COM).

Every effort has been made to contact copyright holders of material reproduced in this book. Any omissions will be rectified in subsequent printings if notice is given to the publisher.

We would like to thank Bill Batson for his invaluable help in the preparation of this book.

Some words are shown in bold, **like this**. You can find out what they mean by looking in the glossary.

# Contents

# Emergency!

High up on an icy mountainside a climber slips and twists his ankle. He can't climb up or down. The wind is howling and it's freezing cold. There's no time to lose. It's time to call for the mountain rescue team!

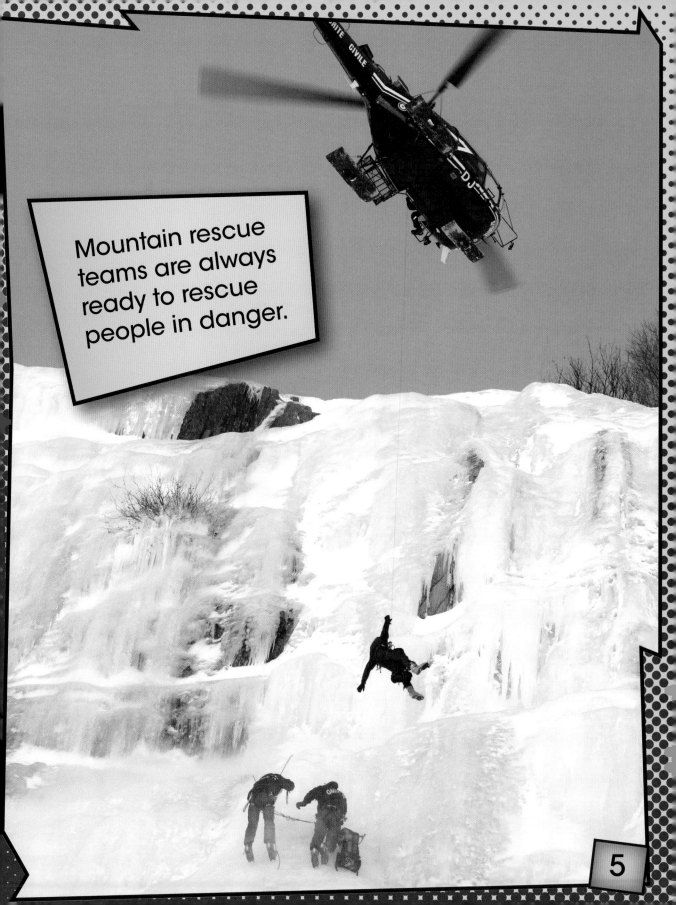

Mountain rescue teams are always ready to rescue people in danger.

# Who needs help?

Hikers, mountaineers, rock climbers, skiers, and forest workers all play and work in the mountains. They need to be rescued if they get lost in bad weather, trapped on a cliff, injured in a fall, or become ill.

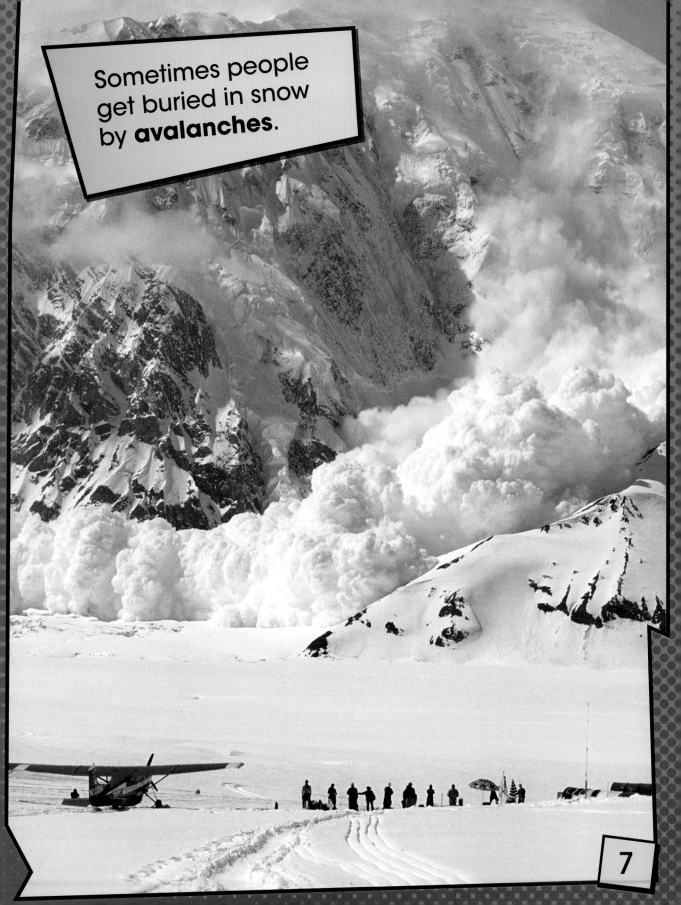

Sometimes people get buried in snow by **avalanches**.

# Meet the team

The members of a mountain rescue team are all expert mountaineers. Some of them are also experts in **first aid**. First aid is help given to an injured or sick person before they are taken to hospital.

**Did you know?**

Mountain rescuers are often **volunteers**. When an emergency call comes they leave their normal jobs and rush to the rescue.

This rescuer is searching for people buried by an **avalanche**.

9

# Helicopter crews

Helicopter crews often help with rescues. Sometimes pilots have to hover just a few metres from cliffs in strong winds. The pilots need to be very skilled to do this.

winch

**Did you know?**
If a pilot can't find a safe place to land, rescuers can be lowered to the ground by a **winch**.

Mountains can be dangerous places. Rescuers often have to climb up and down steep cliffs to reach injured people. The cliffs can be snowy and icy. It's often very windy, with heavy rain or snow, and very cold.

Did you know? Rescuers often have to battle against strong winds at the tops of mountains.

# Mountain rescue equipment

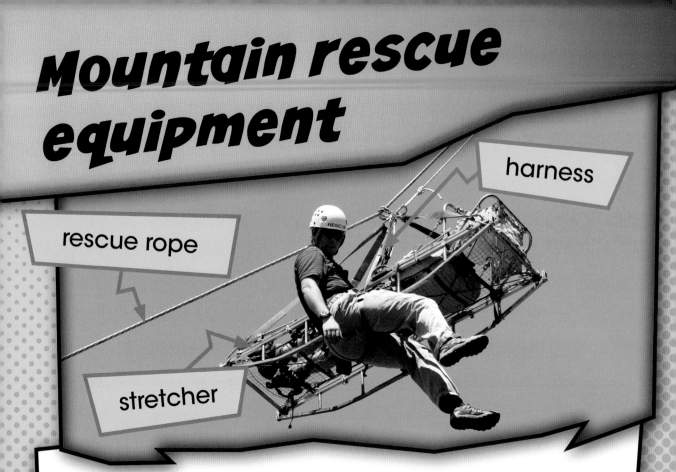

rescue rope

harness

stretcher

Rescue teams need special equipment. They have off-road trucks to travel into the mountains and take injured people to hospital. They carry ropes, **harnesses**, and other equipment to climb cliffs and rescue people. They also stay in touch with each other and their base with walkie-talkie radios.

14

# First aid equipment

Mountain rescue teams always carry a **first aid** kit. They use dressings and bandages to treat cuts and strap up broken bones. They carry medicines to give to people who are sick.

**Did you know?**
Many mountain rescue stretchers come in two parts that can be carried by two people. The parts are put together at the scene.

# Rescue dogs

Dogs often help rescuers. The dogs are specially trained to find people using their sense of smell. They can search the ground much faster than human rescuers can. Dogs can even find people buried under the snow.

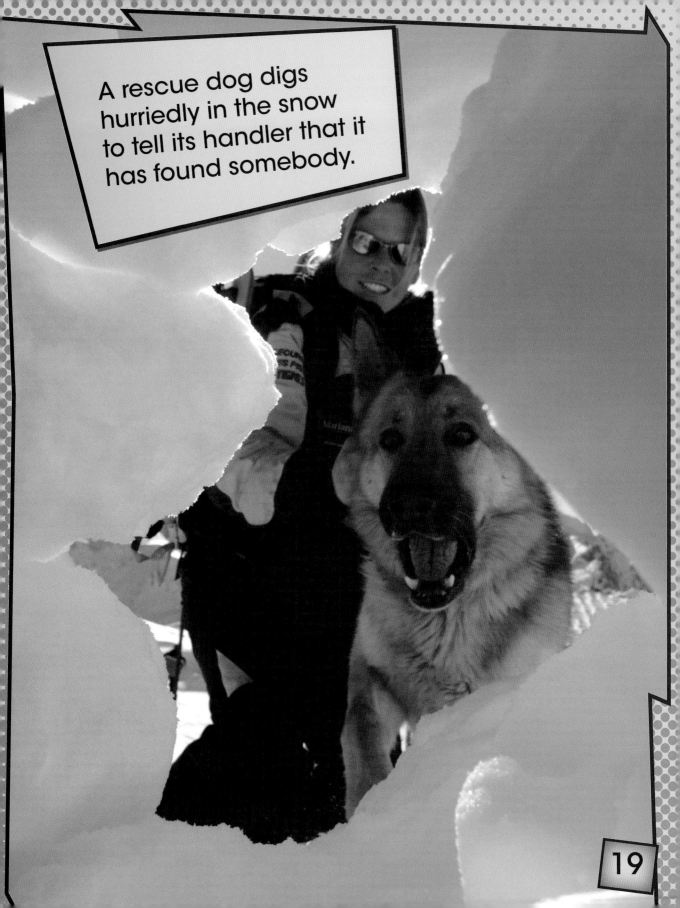

A rescue dog digs hurriedly in the snow to tell its handler that it has found somebody.

# To the rescue!

People who are lost or injured on a mountain call the rescue team by telephone or radio. They tell the team where they are and what injuries they have. The rescue team makes a rescue plan, gathers up their equipment, and sets off for the mountains.

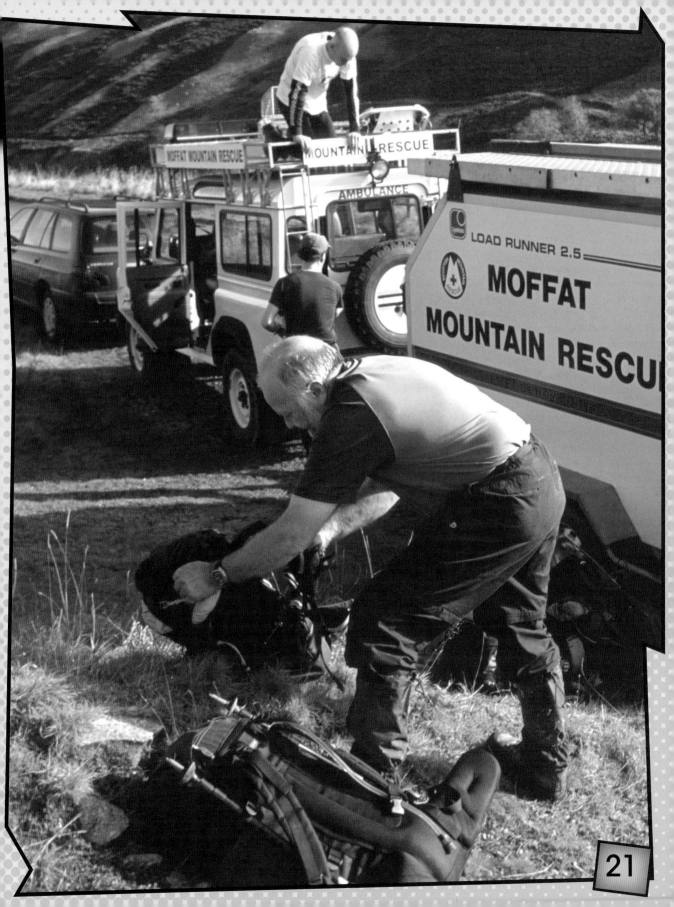

LOAD RUNNER 2.5

MOFFAT
MOUNTAIN RESCUE

MOFFAT MOUNTAIN RESCUE

MOUNTAIN RESCUE

AMBULANCE

21

**Did you know?**
On some rescue helicopters, the injured person is strapped onto a stretcher dangling below the helicopter!

Sometimes people are too ill or badly injured to walk to safety. The rescue team calls in a helicopter to pick up the injured person and take him or her to hospital.

23

# Avalanche rescue

An **avalanche** sweeps away anything in its path. People can end up buried in snow where the avalanche stops. Rescuers sometimes push long sticks called avalanche probes into the snow. If the probe does not hit anything, then no one is buried there.

**Did you know?**
Avalanches can thunder downhill at speeds of more than 350 kilometres per hour.

# Becoming a rescuer

This rescuer is practising first aid on a dummy.

Anybody who wants to be in a mountain rescue team must be an expert mountaineer. Rescuers have to be very fit. They must also know how to find their way in the mountains at night and in bad weather.

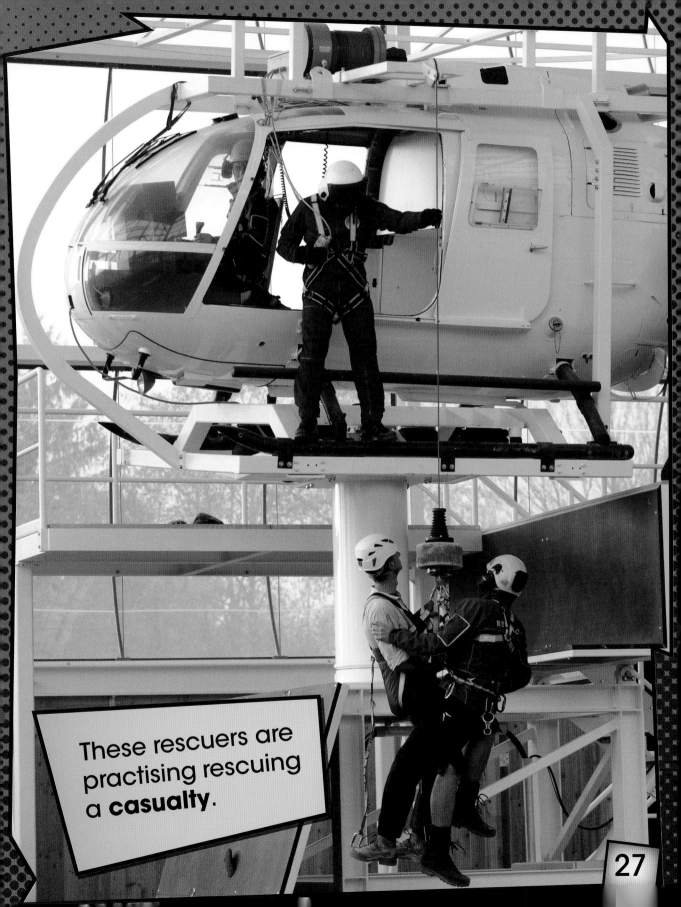

These rescuers are practising rescuing a **casualty**.

# Staying safe in the mountains

Hopefully you will never get into trouble on a mountain. Always follow this simple advice before you set off:

- Never go alone.
- Never go if bad weather is forecast.
- Always take warm clothes.
- Take emergency food and a first aid kit.
- Always tell somebody where you are going and what time you plan to be back.
- In an emergency call for help.

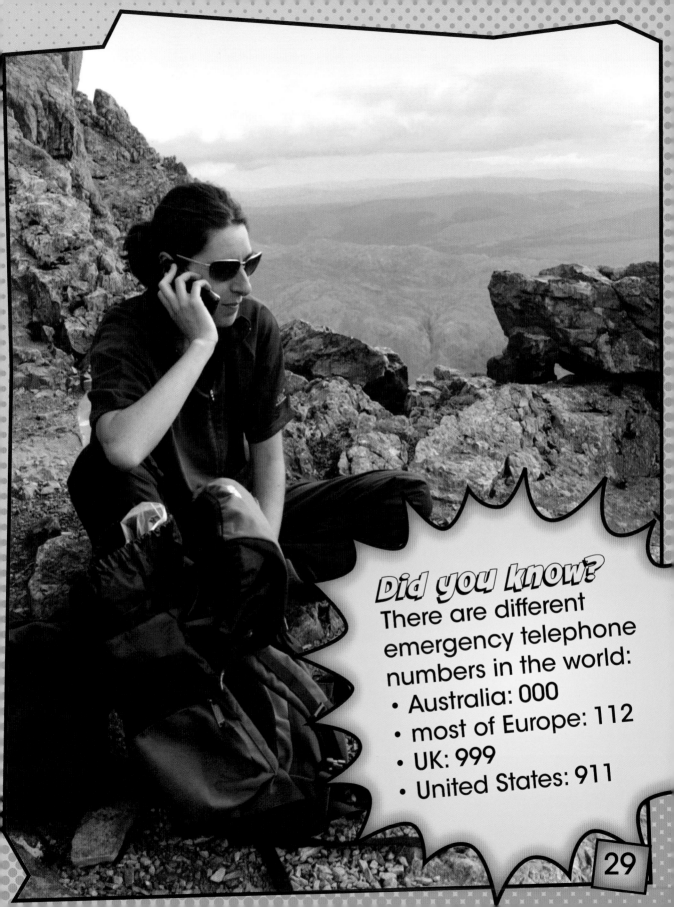

## Did you know?

There are different emergency telephone numbers in the world:

- Australia: 000
- most of Europe: 112
- UK: 999
- United States: 911

# Glossary

**avalanche** huge amount of snow and ice sliding down a mountainside

**casualty** someone who has been injured or killed

**first aid** help given to an injured or sick person before they can be taken to a hospital

**harness** straps that hold a person safely. The person can be picked up by a rope attached to the harness.

**volunteer** somebody who does not get paid for doing a job

**winch** machine that winds in or lets out wire. It can be used to lift people in and out of a helicopter.

# Find out more

## Books

*Helicopters (Machine on the Move)*,
Andrew Langley (Franklin Watts, 2011)

*Mountain Rescue Team*, Jameson Anderson
(Raintree, 2006)

*Paramedic (People Who Help Us series)*,
Rebecca Hunter (Evans Publishing, 2006)

## Websites

**jcsda.com/kids/index.html**
Find out about Search and Rescue dogs with
Hunter, the Search and Rescue dog.

**www.mountain.rescue.org.uk/**
This is the website of Mountain Rescue England
and Wales.

**www.nsarda.org.uk/**
This is the website the UK's National Search and
Rescue Dog Association.

# Index